Billy's Tenth Birthday

JAMES MINTER

HELEN RUSHWORTH - ILLUSTRATOR

ISBN-13: 978-1500749002

ISBN-10: 1500749001

DEDICATION

To those who think bullying and aggression are the way to go through life. They are so wrong …

CONTENTS

ACKNOWLEDGEMENTS

Fiona Joyce, my writing coach, for her usual incisive comments, suggestions and corrections. Helen Rushworth, for her illustrations that so capture the mood of the story. Paul Shinn for his cover design. Maggie, my wife for putting up with my endless pestering to read/comment/discuss my story, and through her work as a personal development coach, her editorial input into the life learnings and their role in becoming a responsible adult.

PREFACE

Life Lessons Book Series

Billy is a child entering young adulthood. He has to make sense of his environment. Like all children, he is confronted with a complex, diverse, fast changing, exciting world full of opportunities, contradictions and dangers through which he must navigate on his way to becoming a responsible adult.

This is a confusing time with a plethora of conflicting information coming from a variety of sources including family, friends, peers, teachers, television and the internet. What underlies Billy's journey, as with all children, is the values he'll adopt. Values provide us with the basis on which we assess the usefulness of what we are told, and how to react to situations we experience; in short, they give us tools to help us forge a path through life. Children's leanings are mostly gained from their parents; becoming a young adult is the time they form values for themselves.

The Life Lessons Series of books were written to have

children form positive values which will serve them at this stage in their life. Each book uses the power of traditional storytelling to illustrate, guide and shape their understanding in a safe environment.

Bullying is a big problem for children today but it is also part of learning to stand up for oneself. In this story Billy, like any other child, is looking forward to a big birthday. However, the local bullies hear he's been given a twenty pound note and challenge him to hand it over. Billy realises he can't fight the gang so has to agree to their demands. At first Billy doesn't dare tell a grownup as he feels guilty about losing it. Billy and his friend Ant try to hatch a plan to get it back. But it's not until Maxine, Ant's sister, hears about the problem that she realises an adult needs to be involved. Grandad who does party magic, is the ideal person to get it back. Max and Grandad hatch a plot. The bullies don't realise what is happening until it's too late. Grandad recovers the twenty pound note leaving the bullies bemused.

Disarming a bully is the better way of dealing with them. You can't rid the world of bullies but you can do something about how you deal with them.

1 - TEN TEN TEN MUST BE MAGIC

To be ten years old, on the tenth day, of the tenth month, has to be magical. The thought raced through Billy's mind. He clapped his hands in excitement.

'Ten, ten, ten, Jacko.'

At the mention of his name Jacko wagged his tail.

'I've only a week to go before my birthday.'

Jacko continued licking his paw. He didn't share Billy's enthusiasm.

'This birthday is special; it's never to be repeated … ever.' Billy looked at his dog. 'Are you listening to me?'

Jacko licked his hand.

'Do you know what Jacko? I can count to over a thousand and spell marmalade.'

The Golden Retriever didn't look impressed.

'I can do all sorts of stuff now, so what's it going to be like when I'm ten? You know Ant?'

At the mention of Billy's best mate's name Jacko's tail was off again.

'He can't spell London. I can. Everyone but everyone, knows there are two *on's* in London and no *no's*. Even his sister Max knows, and she's only eight.'

Hearing Max's name Jacko moved closer to Billy's bed. He pushed his nose under the covers.

'Yes I know you like Max. She's coming to my birthday party. As Ant's sister we don't want to leave her out. But Mum said she won't count her as one of my six friends.'

'I'm inviting Anthony, I mean Ant ... Do you know why I call him Ant?' Billy looked to the dog but he didn't answer. 'Because it's quicker to say. If we're in trouble, it can be the difference between being caught and looking totally innocent. Old Ticker Wright never catches us on his police bike as we pedal quicker. He's nice really.'

Jacko remained indifferent.

'Mum and Dad are getting me a new big bike so I can ride even faster. It's what I want. But when other people buy me things they never get it right. Not because they don't try but more because I'm not exactly sure what I want'.

Jacko's head disappeared under the duvet. Billy lifted it to see what he was up to.

'Seeing something on TV or on the internet and holding it in your hand is different. I've made that mistake before. Grandad never buys what I want. Mum says I should be grateful for whatever I'm given'.

Jacko caught the hem of Billy's pyjama leg in his teeth and pulled.

Billy looked down at him. 'You're easy to buy for. A big bone and you're happy for hours. I did say to Grandad *I think it would be better if you gave me money.* It sort of slipped out before I was able to stop the words. I didn't mean to hurt his feelings.'

Jacko wasn't listening, he tugged on the pyjama leg; Billy tugged back. He guessed Jacko wanted to go downstairs and outside for a walk.

'In a minute ... Actually Grandad looked pleased when I asked for money. Toyshops and department stores aren't his thing.'

Jacko tugged harder. Billy tugged back; Jacko let go slumping down to rest his head on his paws.

Billy continued, 'Mum wasn't so happy. She said I was

being cheeky and her dad tried his best. Then she said, remembering some of the presents he'd bought her, she understood.' Billy swung his legs out of bed. 'Come on then!'

2 - BILLY'S TENTH BIRTHDAY

The Saturday of Billy's birthday arrived. It was half-term as well. His alarm woke him seven. He wasn't going to miss the postman or give Jacko a chance to eat any of his cards.

Alerted by the *clink-clank* sound of the letterbox he slipped out from under his Transformers duvet, grabbing his red stripy dressing gown off the floor.

Jumping into his slippers—they were the sort with no backs—he made a running stumbling descent of the stairs. Unhurt he was just in time to rugby-tackle Jacko who was racing down the hall towards the front door, the letter box, and anything protruding through it. A seven stone Goldie, travelling at speed, takes some holding. Billy, now 10, found extra strength matching his double figure age. He restrained the dog before anything was sniffed, chewed, slobbered on, or swung violently left and right in a frenzied bout of destruction. Instead of being annoyed, Jacko turned and gave him a good licking, followed by a beating with his full brush tail. History had shown his tail was capable of clearing a low coffee table of all its contents with no regard for fragility, sentiment or value—all items went the same way.

Billy shuffled through the post. He plucked out an envelope.

'Look Jacks, this is mine!' Quite clearly the one marked *Master W Field* belonged to him. Although his dad was Walter, he was well past being a 'Master'. Anyway Grandad was always so precise, Billy knew this card came from him. He'd posted it even though he lived just two streets away, next door but one to Ant. Three other envelopes were addressed to him. One just had Billy scribbled across it in two inch high blue felt-tip writing. *Ant without doubt. He's never up this early even on a school day,* thought Billy. *He must have got his dad to deliver it on his way to work.*

He laid the four unopened cards on the breakfast table. Then he sorted and stacked them into order, the top one to be opened first, the bottom one last.

Saving the best for last, was a saying he remembered. Which one should be last was easy to decide. Grandad always chose great cards, and he was his only grandad, making him doubly special. Next were two cards from his two aunties. They were twins. He didn't see them often.

On top was Ant's card. There was no present as he would bring it to the party, but Ant always wrote a joke inside his cards. He didn't fail this time: *What goes up but never comes down?*

Billy tossed the card to one side, 'Everyone knows that; it's your age!'

Billy held up his aunts' cards. 'Look at these two Jacko. They might be twins but they were born in different months. Aunty May was born on the 31st May, just before midnight and Aunty June was born thirty minutes later. Something like that happening is as crazy as my ten, ten, ten birthday.' Billy fished out a gift voucher from each envelop. 'Mum says it's because they live in Devon. Apparently the postage cost of a present would be too much. Though Mum thinks that's a cop-out.' *Why don't they just send one card and one gift voucher. It would be cheaper.* Billy thought.

Jacko sniffed at the cards.

'Can you smell cats?' He brought the cards nearer to Jacko. 'They share their house with fourteen at the last count.'

Pouring milk over his Sugar Puffs, Billy had left the best card until last. Picking up Grandad's card he held it towards the light, hoping to get a hint of the contents. *Money, money, money* went through his mind.

'Please let it be money.' Taking a spoonful of cereal he

dribbled milk down his chin. A quick wipe and it was gone. Dressing gown sleeves were designed for such emergencies.

He grabbed the breadknife. Holding the blade away from him, he inched it along the envelope's seal. He didn't want to damage the money inside. Peering into the slit, he could make out a cartoon style drawing. Pulling out the card he saw it was a picture of a boy on a bicycle, wobbling along a pot holed track.

He opened it. No money. 'Oh Jacko,' his heart sank. 'I knew it.'

Confused and disappointed, he dropped the card and ran for his bedroom.

Jacko took up the chase. He beat Billy to the bottom of

the stairs and raced for the top. Four legs being better than two, he arrived first. He sat, tongue lolling, waiting for slow coach to catch up.

As Billy's face levelled he tried to lick him, but Billy moved him gently aside. He went into his bedroom and threw himself on his bed. Jacko slunk after him, waiting until he'd settled before climbing up beside him.

'Happy birthday Billy!' his mum called. Her head appeared at his bedroom door, 'Why the long face?' She creased her brow. 'You've been waiting for today for ages, what's happened?' She sat on his bed. He rolled over, burying his face in the pillow. She stroked his hair. 'Billy,' she lowered her voice, 'talk to me.'

'Grandad,' he whispered. He pressed his face into the pillow.

Jacko sneezed as dogs do for no apparent reason. They both jumped. Billy stretched his arm out to smooth the dog's fur, but said nothing.

'What about Grandad? What's he done?' Mum asked.

'No money.'

'What do you mean no money?'

'It'll be some stupid present like usual … I asked him for money.'

'Billy you can't make demands on him. People give presents because they want to, not because you asked. You don't know what he's got you. It'll be a surprise.' She sounded cheery trying to lift his spirits. 'You know you like surprises. What about …'

The hollow feeling in his stomach remained. 'Mum,' he cut her off, 'it's just 'cos he's old. He has no idea what kids want.' He buried his face back in the pillow.

'Be that as it may, you'd better buck up young man! You've got guests arriving in a few hours for your party.' She tried to lift him into a sitting position but failed. He was a dead weight. Jacko jumped off the bed in anticipation.

'Okay Jacko I'm coming.' She stroked his head. 'Now Billy, shower and downstairs as quick as you can … And no more Mr. Grumpy!'

3 - THE BIRTHDAY PARTY

'It's three-o-clock.' No sooner had Billy spoken than the doorbell rang, followed by three hard raps of the knocker.

'Okay, keep your hair on.' Billy and Jacko reached the door together. 'Hi mate, I should have known it was you.'

Ant gave Jacko a stroke as he passed; Max was behind. Seeing Jacko she got onto her knees to give him a hug. He licked her face.

'Oi I've had a wash today!' She wiped her cheek with her sleeve.

The house reeled to the sound of six boys, one girl and one dog having fun. Blind man's buff proved popular as did musical chairs. Sticking the tail on the donkey, with Jacko as the donkey, took on a new twist. Blindfolded, with an arm behind their backs, each child took it in turns to Sellotape a cardboard tail onto a boisterous dog with little understanding of, or regard for, the game's rules.

'Okay, listen up,' Billy's mum clapped her hands to get their attention, 'If you go into the next room.' She raised her voice against the noise. 'Boys, hush now! We have our entertainer. The Great Magisco!' She threw open her arms like the curtains of a theatre unfolding. 'The Great Magisco will perform tricks the likes of which you've never seen before!' The drama in her voice got the children's attention.

In the sitting room they settled on the floor. The curtains were pulled shut. When Mum turned off a small table lamp it went dark. The boys whistled and hooted.

Music began. Low and haunting. Then louder. As it reached a crescendo the lights came on and, as if by magic, The Great Magisco appeared.

Actually it was Grandad, in a top hat from Oxfam and a green plastic cape he used to keep the rain off while fishing. He was twirling a black walking stick.

He bowed deeply, and with such force his hat toppled forward. Quick as a flash he caught it. He held out both hat and stick to his assistant standing alongside. Max, in a pink tutu covered in sequins, sparkled as she moved.

The music faded. The Great Magisco spoke:

'I hope you're here in good cheer,

To see and wonder at sights to behold,

Magic is serious, magic is fun but most of all,

It has to be done with no disbelievers I'm told.'

He raised his finger and pointed at Billy and his friends. 'Do you believe in magic?'

Each boy nodded, except Tom who laughed.

'So I see we have a doubter … Boy would you like me to turn you into a frog?

Tom stopped laughing while the others roared. 'Shush and we'll begin.' The Great Magisco beckoned to Max. She passed him a pack of playing cards. He shuffled them twice, making large, elaborate gestures. The boys, silent and unblinking, watched.

Shaping the cards into a fan, Magisco offered the pack to each boy in turn. 'One card each', he instructed.

'Now don't show your card to me or anyone else. Take a look for yourself and then sit on it.' His voice was ferocious, almost a growl. Billy had never heard him speak like this. Jacko wandered up to Max looking for reassurance.

She tried to shove him away. 'I'm busy silly. It's okay its only grandad you old softy.'

The Great Magisco passed the remaining cards to his sequinned assistant. As he did so, Jacko pushed his nose between Max's hands and the approaching pack. The whole lot landed on the carpet. All the boys laughed.

'You've spoilt it now.' Max told Jacko. He looked at her with his large brown soulful eyes. 'Go on – shoo' she said gently.

Billy half rose and called to Jacko. His mum stood behind him; he didn't know why. Jacko ignored them both. Billy had to stand and pat his knees to get him to come. 'Sit!' he told him. Jacko groaned as he sat. Billy squatted beside him. They both faced the stage.

Magisco made a knot in a piece of rope. He shook the rope and the knot vanished. Everyone gasped and clapped. He made a coin disappear, only to reappear behind Ant's ear. More gasps and clapping.

'Now for my last trick.'

The lights dimmed. Max rolled a newspaper into a long thin tube. Mum turned the lights up again and now Max tipped the tube every which way so all could see it was empty.

Passing it to The Great Magisco, he twirled around swishing his cape for effect.

'Abracadabra, see them fly. Watch the balls take to the sky.' Bringing the tube to his mouth he made a mighty huff. Two ping pong balls shot to the far side of the room.

One of them bounced off a picture frame. Ant caught it.

The other dropped down behind the sofa. Hot on its trail Jacko squeezed into an impossible gap. True to his breed, he sniffed and snorted in the dust until he retrieved it.

Magisco took Max's hand. They bowed.

'That's all … except to sing happy birthday to Billy.' Grandad smiled at him. 'Maybe we should all stand up to sing.'

All the boys stood.

'Here what's that?' Tom pointed at the floor behind Billy. 'There behind you Billy … on the floor.'

'Yeah, yeah, very good, I'm not falling for that.' Billy said. But he couldn't help taking a sneak peak. He took a sharp intake of breath. 'Wow! A twenty pound note lay where he had been squatting.

'Grandad look!' He waved the note over his head. 'Your magic, it worked … My cards gone, but see what I've got.' He ran to his Grandad and clasped both arms around him. He held on with great force. Grandad rocked to and fro.

'Steady on. You'll have me over. I'm not as young as I used to be.' Grandad hugged him back. 'Isn't that what you wanted?'

'You're the best grandad ever. Thanks.'

'Now don't lose it. Put it up in your bedroom safe, away from Jacko.'

On hearing his name Jacko appeared with a mouthful of red and black striped sock, fluff, and ping pong ball. Looking proud of himself he waited for praise but Billy was gone.

His first ever twenty pound note, for his tenth birthday, on the tenth day of the tenth month, from his only grandad! He needed to make sure no one took it. Or if they did, he wanted be certain it was his. He wrote his name on it in black ink: BILLY followed by 10 10 10.

4 - BILLY AND ANT AT THE PARK

'Now be careful Billy; keep off the main road. And remember, walk over the crossing. Traffic moves too fast near the park. You'd think they'd put speed bumps in.' His mum's voice trailed away.

Once inside the park gates Billy and Ant practiced wheelies every time the coast was clear.

'This bike's awesome.' Billy was really happy with his present.

'Oi Field, I hear you had a birthday party. Why didn't you invite me?' Someone shouted.

Billy stopped dead.

'Ant here, quick.' He held his hand to his mouth so only Ant could hear. 'That's Tom's older brother Eddy isn't it?'

Ant peered across at the three lads standing next to the swings. 'Looks like him but I've on idea who he's with. I don't think we should go any nearer.'

'Didn't you hear me?' Eddy walked towards them, his mates tagging along behind. 'I said you had a birthday party and didn't invite me. I think that's a bit rude.' His pace quickened.

'He invited people from our class. Your brother Tom came.' Ant called back.

'I ain't talking to you titch.' Eddy poked Ant in the chest. 'It's birthday boy here I've a problem with.' He stared hard at Billy. 'My brother says you had a magician and you got a twenty pound note from your grandad. Well I like magic. Too bad I ain't got a grandad. He died. I think you ought to give that twenty pound note to me … 'cos you feel sorry for my loss.' He pressed his face up to Billy's. His breath smelt stale from mint gum and cigarettes. Billy pulled back. His bike shifted off balance, he nearly dropped it.

'Mind my trainers with that heap.' Eddy kicked the tyre. 'See what you've done! There's a big black mark right across the front.' He lifted his foot to show them.

Billy felt a lump in his throat. He'd never liked Eddy, and liked him even less now.

'But you did that. You just kicked my tyre!' Billy spoke before thinking.

'You calling me a liar?' Eddy turned to his mates for support, 'Did you hear him?' As he spoke he poked Billy's arm.

His mates nodded in agreement.

'What you going to do about it Eddy?' the tallest one asked.

'I think I need to teach him a lesson in manners. A hard lesson. It's not nice to go around calling people liars. Didn't your mother teach you nothing? You have got a mother haven't you? Oh that's right, she's that Deputy Head Teacher.

A right old bag she is—always barking at us. Do this, don't do that. Doesn't she drive you crazy at home?' Eddy laughed and so did his mates.

'I saw you kick the tyre.' Ant said. He pulled himself up to his full height. 'My mate did nothing.'

'You again. When I want your opinion I'll ask for it.' Eddy held him in a stare. 'My beef is with birthday boy, not you, unless you want a slap as well.' Ant held Eddy's stare. Then he dropped his eyes and stepped back a pace. He looked at a spot on the ground.

'I'll tell you what Billy Field, if you get on your bike now!' Eddy shouted the *now,* 'And ride back to your house to fetch me your twenty quid, I'll forget all about this.' He didn't wait for an answer. He looked at his watch. 'Be at the bottom of your road in fifteen minutes. Go on get out of here! What are you waiting for? The clock's ticking.' He swung at Billy trying to slap him around the back of his head. He missed. Billy and Ant pedalled away for all they were worth. The sound of laughter accompanied their retreat.

'What are we going to do Billy?' Ant puffed. They kept up the pace.

'I've got no choice. When we get back to my place say nothing to my mum or dad, and especially not to Grandad if you see him.

'But you can't say nothing; what if your mum asks what you've done with the money?'

They pulled up outside Billy's house. 'Just follow my lead.'

'That was quick boys. Nothing wrong is there? You haven't got a puncture or anything like that.' Billy's mum looked at each of them in turn.

'No nothing Mum, I just forgot something that's all. We're off out again in a minute.' Billy passed straight through the kitchen, trailed by Ant. Jacko joined in the procession.

The boys made their way to Billy's bedroom, where Billy collected his twenty pound note from his wooden pencil case where he had hidden it and pushed in his pocket. They marched straight back downstairs again, through the kitchen, to the back door.

Jacko followed on, believing he was going with them.

'Sorry mate.' Billy stopped to give him a rub. Bending down he whispered in his ear, 'I bet you could have him.' He stroked Jacko one more time. As he did so a tear trickled into the corner of his eye. The thought of giving up his twenty pound note struck home.

'You alright Billy? You look like you're crying.' Mum

noticed.

'Mum! Of course not. It's just one of Jacko's hairs jabbed me in the eye.' He rubbed it.

As they approached the end of their road Billy saw the group of older boys.

'There they are.' He pointed. Ant being smaller couldn't see over the cars until they were closer.

'Oh yeah, I see him now. What are we going to do?' He looked to Billy for guidance.

'You stop before we reach them and turn around for a quick getaway. I'll pedal on, fling the note at Eddy, then keep going as fast as I can. If we split up they can't chase us both. Billy looked to Ant to make sure he'd understood. Ant returned his glance.

'Okay go straight home and we'll meet up as soon as we can.'

Billy drew alongside the boys. He hit his brakes hard. They screeched in response. A dust cloud hovered around the back tyre before fading. He halted for a split second, long enough to stuff the note into Eddy's hand. Desperate to get away he pushed hard on his pedals. Watching for any flailing hands or feet, he ducked passed the three older boys to make good his escape.

He pushed so hard his foot slipped off the pedal. The bike lurched to one side. Billy lay in a heap. He saw Eddy start moving towards him. Without hesitation and ignoring the pain from his shin, he scrambled back onto his bike.

'Right Billy boy you've not seen the last of me. Run scaredy-cat but don't forget I know where you live!' Eddy's voice followed him as he made good his get away.

5 - ANT TELLS MAX

Ant reached his house unscathed. Max was playing in the garden.

'Where's Billy? she said. 'I thought you two were on a bike ride? I saw his new bike at his party. It was in the garage. I would have a yellow one. That's the colour of the sun; all bright and cheery. Colours should be cheerful, yellow makes you happy.' She stopped talking to catch her breath. 'Are you happy?' She looked into Ant's face as he walked past. 'You don't look happy. I'm happy. Why aren't all people happy? What's to be sad about?' She skipped down the path.

'Max just shut up. His bike's blue. So what?'

She shrugged her shoulders. 'I was only saying yellow's like the sun. Anyway don't shout at me. It's not nice to shout. I've done nothing wrong.'

'Sorry sis. It's just Billy and me had a bit of trouble at the park.'

'What? Who with?' She stopped smiling.

'Tom's brother Eddy.'

'What old stupid Eddy?'

'Shush don't let him hear you say that.' Ant looked around to make sure no one had heard, 'He nicked Billy's twenty pound note; the one his grandad magicked.'

'Why?'

'Cos Billy never invited him to his party. He was especially bothered, as he likes magic.'

'Well his sister Kate, she's in my class, always calls him

stupid. Apparently he smokes around the back of the bike sheds and everyone knows smoking is stupid. So he must be.'

'Are you good friends with Kate?'

'She's my …' Max counted on her fingers, 'my number six best friend. No wait, me and Sally fell out 'cos she told Miss I cheated in spelling. I didn't really. It just happened I had *danger* written on my hand from where I was learning words for our test. So Kate's my one, two, three, four, five best friend.'

'Fifth not five.'

'That's what I said.' She held her hand up with all fingers pointing upwards. 'See its five.'

'Fine five. Will you see Kate before the end of half-term?'

'Maybe. There's swimming club tomorrow. She's usually there. Why?'

'We need a plan to get Billy's money back before his grandad finds out it's been stolen.'

'Well she told me that on Tuesday, her, Tom and Eddy are all going to town to shop for school uniform stuff. Their mum's taking them. Maybe you and Billy could learn to be pick-pockets like in Oliver Twist. You could bump into Eddy when he's with his mum, and steal it back.' She beamed.

6 - MAX HAS A PLAN

'Ah my magic helper! I wondered who was knocking at my door.' Billy's grandad tousled Max's hair.

'Please Billy's grandad, I need to tell you something.' Max looked around to check no one was listening.

'Well don't stand there, come on in. Only for a few minutes mind. I'm off to Billy's house for tea. We'll probably have leftovers from the party. Curly sandwiches and stale cake. I think my daughter believes I'm a dustbin. It's true I hate waste. As my dad would say, *waste not, want not.* We had none of this recycling malarkey in my day. Nobody ever left anything! Most of the time there wasn't enough to go round, never mind waste it.' He sat down in his large armchair. Max sat on the sofa. 'So what's so important young lady?'

'Billy doesn't know I'm here, nor does Ant, but I have a

plan to get the money back.' She covered her mouth with her hand, fearful of being overheard.

'Hold on … a plan … money back? What are you talking about?' His brow furrowed.

'You know Eddy, Tom's older brother and Kate, his sister who's in my class, well he, that's Eddy, not Tom of course, …'

'No of course' He bent forward hoping to improve his concentration.

'... stole the twenty pounds you magicked to Billy. And I have a plan to get it back.' She looked at him as if to say, *isn't it obvious?*

Leaning forward hadn't help. He scratched his head.

'Am I hearing you right? Are you saying Billy's had his present stolen by this Eddy boy?'

'Yes'

He shook his head in disbelief. 'What's the world coming to?'

'Eddy's fourteen, nearly fifteen and he goes to Elliot's where Billy's mum is the head teacher.'

'Deputy Head Teacher but anyway; does she know about

Eddy? And does she know you're here?'

'My mum knows I'm here, but I told her it was about magic. She doesn't know about the lost money, no one does.

'Lost or stolen? There's a big difference.' He rubbed his chin. 'Did Billy lose it and did Eddy find it?'

'Not according to Ant. He said Eddy stole it when they were over the park.' She looked to see if he'd understood. 'So I suggested they pick-pocket Eddy on Tuesday when he's in town with Kate and Tom buying school uniform stuff. Well I'm not sure what they're buying, but his mum will be there. Then I thought of your magic, so that's why I'm here …' She flopped back on the sofa relieved to have completed her story.

'Hmm magic you say.' He rubbed his hand around the back of his neck. 'What is your plan exactly?'

'Well Ant said Eddy took the money 'cos he wasn't invited to the party and he missed the magic.' Max pulled a folded sheet of paper from her pocket. 'Here.' She held up a drawing, 'It's not finished but it won't take long. I need to do some more colouring.' She waved it about a bit, then held it in front of Grandad for him to see.

'And what is this?' Grandad was more confused than ever, but he didn't want to dampen her enthusiasm.

'I've only done it from memory but it's a twenty pound note. Look there's the two and there's the nothing.' Her finger darted between the two figures.

'It's a nought, not nothing.'

Now Max looked confused.

'Oh it doesn't matter. So you're suggesting we take your twenty pound note and swap it for the real thing?'

'Using your magic! Like you made the card turn into money. That way Billy gets his money back and Eddy …'

'…ends up with a drawing. You're not expecting him to think it's an actual twenty pound note are you?'

'No course not. It's to teach him a lesson.'

'And this will happen Tuesday you say.'

'Yeah. Tomorrow I'm seeing Kate.'

'Not Tuesday?'

'At swimming; it's always swimming club on Monday.'

He felt his understanding ebbing away.

'Billy's grandad you need to concentrate …' She waited for the lines on his forehead to smooth before continuing. 'At swimming I'll ask Kate if I can go with her and her mum shopping on Tuesday. You come to town too. The uniform shop is in the shopping centre. I'll meet you under the clock, the one where all those soldiers march around swinging their guns.' Her face lit up at the thought, 'I'll come and find you.'

'I know the clock. I've taken Billy there many times … Then what?' He looked at her expectantly.

'We'll find Eddy, then you make the money jump out of his pocket or something.' She shrugged her shoulders. 'I don't know, you're the one who does magic.'

'I think I need to give your plan more thought. But I'll meet you under the clock alright. Right now I'm afraid, I have to get ready to go to tea.' He stood.

Max slipped down from the sofa. 'Don't say nothing to Billy. Ant says he's very upset and it wasn't his fault. It was stupid Eddy's.'

I wonder how stupid Eddy really is, Grandad thought, He opened the door for Max. 'Bye. Mum's the word.' He waved to her. 'Straight home now. See you in the shopping centre at midday …'

When Billy woke on Monday morning his mum was in her study surrounded by piles of paper not wanting to be disturbed. He sat at the kitchen table and played with his cereal, moving it around the bowl. His eyes felt puffy from a night of crying. He pushed all the cereal to one side of the bowl and took a spoonful of sugary milk. He pushed at the cereal again with his spoon. Jacko sat watching him.

'It's not fair.' Jacko licked his hand. 'You watch when I'm older I'll have him.' The full length body strokes Billy gave Jacko now were more out of frustration than love. 'What can I do?'

Jacko yawned.

'Sorry mate, am I boring you?' Sarcasm was lost on the dog. 'You sure you've got no ideas? And don't say tell Mum or Dad. I can't. If I do Grandad'll find out.' He fought hard to hold back tears. 'I hate that Eddy.'

Ant's face appeared at the kitchen window; jacket collar pulled up against the morning chill. He tapped on the glass. 'Come on, its blinking freezing out here.'

'It's unlocked.' Billy's voice sounded like a feeble old man. Ant let himself in and started speaking straightaway.

'I've been thinking about what Max said. You know, about becoming pick-pockets. I tried it on her and got a sweet. She never felt a thing.' Ant pulled himself up to full height. 'It's all about distraction.' A smile filled his face. 'Go on stand up.'

Ant pushed on Billy's shoulder, 'I'll show you. Come on.' Ant had created his own drawing of a twenty pound note. He passed it to him. 'Put that in your pocket.'

Billy stood by the kitchen table, Ant walked towards him acting all cool. He banged into his shoulder, 'Oh sorry mate.' He fumbled around trying to get his fingers into Billy's trouser pocket. Jacko pushed between them, defending his master. Both boys started to laugh.

'If you do that to Eddy Jost you won't be laughing for long.' Billy stopped, he dropped his head. 'Any other ideas?'

'Not really. But Max said Tom, Kate and Eddy are in town tomorrow with their mum. Max is going with Kate to see the clock. You know the one with the soldiers.' Ant waited for a response.

'So …?' Billy couldn't be bothered to speak.

'If we go maybe we can tell Eddy's mum what he did and she'll get it back for us.'

Billy curled his top lip.

Ant was desperate to help his mate. 'I know it's not great. And maybe she won't believe us. But I'm not sure we've any other option.'

7 - THE GREAT MAGISCO

'Come on Mum, I'm not a kid. I've seen that clock loads of times. Those stupid soldiers marching about. Do I have to?' Eddy protested.

'You're not the only one in this family; Kate and Tom want to see it … and Max I imagine. If we don't hurry we'll miss it striking twelve.'

Eddy pushed Tom. 'Baby brother wants to see the soldiers.'

'Hey enough of that; you were always on at me to take you to see it.' His mum glared at him.

'Yeah, when I was five maybe. I'll be fifteen next month.'

'Well you're still my baby.' She grabbed his cheek. 'Coochy coo.'

‘Oi get off.’ He jerked his head away.

‘We’re going to get lunch after seeing the clock; I suppose you’re not too big to eat with us?’ She thought food would win him over.

‘No thanks, I’m meeting my mates at twelve. We’re off for a burger.’ He hooked his fingers into the waistband of his jeans, pulling them up enough to cover his boxers.

‘Oh okay. So where are you getting the money from?’

Eddy dropped his gaze focusing on the floor. He shuffled his feet. The clock came into view; several people were gathered underneath it. Eddy saw his mates standing off to one side making out they weren’t particularly interested.

‘Well?’

He mumbled something about a paper round and mooched off.

Max spotted Billy’s grandad. ‘Billy’s grandad!’ she called. I’m here! She ran in front and reached him just as the clock struck twelve.

On each strike a different door in the clock face opened. Large carved wooden figures dressed in red tunics, black trousers and boots moved forward to present arms. The intricate mechanism whirred and chattered as soldier followed soldier, moving around an elaborate track, before disappearing again for another twelve hours.

Kate's mum, Kate, and Tom, came to stand by Max. 'This is Billy's grandad'. Max said. 'He does magic.'

'I know Tom here.' Grandad shook Tom's hand. 'This young man said he didn't believe in magic. But I think he changed his mind.' He smiled at Tom.

Tom smiled back.

'Max said she was meeting you here.' Kate's mum looked to Grandad for confirmation.

'She's my assistant. We've an important trick to perform.' Grandad put his arm round Max's shoulder. She beamed up at him.

'We're going to get some lunch first.' Max said. She had her eye on Eddy who was standing several feet away talking to his mates. 'Quick, we need to go. This way.' She pulled on Grandad's jacket. 'Bye Kate!' Grandad said goodbye to the others. They moved off. Neither saw Ant and Billy arrive with Jacko on a lead.

‘Can you bend down?’ Max put her mouth close to his ear. ‘I heard them say they’re going to get a burger. We need to catch them up.’ Still holding Grandad’s jacket she led the way.

Eddy and his mates were close to the front door of the burger bar.

‘Which one is Eddy?’ Grandad peered at the group of teenage boys.

‘Him … the one with his jeans hanging down.’

‘He needs a belt by the look of it.’

‘Billy’s grandad don’t be silly; that’s the fashion.’

‘Well not for me it’s not. Trousers are worn at the waist.’

‘Come on they’ve gone in here.’ Max went first. They joined the queue behind the lads close enough to eavesdrop.

‘It’s your treat Eddy mate since you nicked the money.’

‘I didn’t exactly nick it … he sort of gave it to me.’ All the boys laughed.

‘Yeah, otherwise you’d have given him a beating.’ More laughter followed.

‘So where’s this famed twenty pound note?’ Another of the lads asked.

'Hope he shows it.' Max whispered standing on tip-toe trying to see.

Grandad shushed her, 'He'll hear.'

Eddy slapped his thigh.

Without warning, Max reached up to tap Eddy's arm. He spun around. First he looked to Billy's grandad and then at her.

'What?'

'You said you like magic.' Max said.

'Who wants to know?'

Grandad took over the conversation. 'I heard you like magic and were upset at not being invited to Billy Field's party.'

'What are you on about?' Eddy looked them up and down, then turned back to his mates.

Grandad tapped his shoulder. 'What my assistant and I are trying to say is we hear you like magic so we're here to do a trick for you.'

Eddy turned to look at him. 'Pull the other one old man it's got bells on.' He turned back to his mates. 'This bloke's off his rocker.'

The queue moved forward. Soon they'd have to order and pay for their meals. Max tugged at Grandad's jacket. 'Go on now before it's too late.'

'So Eddy.' Eddy turned back to face them. 'You've a twenty pound note.'

'Who told you? Mind your own business.' He said. He looked around to see who might be listening. Max saw his leg begin to shake.

'Would you like another one … for free?' Grandad asked him.

'What, you'd give me twenty quid for nothing? You're having me on.'

'No not at all. It's magic.'

'If I say *yes* will you go away?' He laughed at his own statement. His mates joined in.

'For sure. The trick won't take long. All I need is your twenty pound note.' He looked into Eddy's eyes. 'You do trust me don't you?'

'What, an old bloke like you?' He stared back, unsure of what was going to happen. 'Here.' Eddy dug into his pocket to retrieve the crumpled note. 'Let's see what you can do with that … mind you, I want it back.'

Max slipped her hand-drawn note to grandad and he slid it up his sleeve. Taking the real note from Eddy he held it up for all to see.

'My, the Queen wouldn't be happy to see what you've done to her currency.' Using slow, deliberate movements he proceeded to smooth it out. Then he held it over his head.

The queue was restless. Shouts of 'Come on move up,' and 'I'm hungry,' followed.

Unperturbed The Great Magisco pivoted left and right showing off the note to anyone who cared to look. He made a growling noise, it came from deep in his chest.

He whispered to Max, 'When I say *now,* grab my hand and we'll make a dash for it.' She smiled and nodded to show she'd heard. 'Abracadabra.' He waved his hands around. 'On the head of my mother … let this note turn into another!' He pushed his hands upwards and outwards.

He let Max's drawing fly. It rose into the air above Eddy's head. All eyes turned to watch it.

'Now!' Grandad grabbed Max's outstretched hand and fled. He held her hand tight as they ran for the burger bar exit.

Outside they sprinted towards the clock.

'I'm a fast runner.' She could hear him panting. 'Are you okay?'

'We're … nearly … there.' He breathed heavily. 'There's the clock.' He looked about. 'Can you see Kate's mum anywhere?' He stopped to scan the various eating places. She wasn't visible.

'Come on Grandad. Look who I can see over there …' Max pointed to two policemen browsing in a shop window. 'It's Ticker Wright! He's often in our street.' She clapped her hands in glee. 'He always gives me a sweet. They're hard brown ones with black lines. Humberts or something.'

'Why do you call him Ticker Wright?' Grandad panted. He was curious.

'Oh, it's his bike. It makes a tick, tick noise as he rides up the street.' She ran towards the policemen.

Grandad slowed to a stop. Propped up against a wall he held his chest. He struggled for breath. He felt unwell.

'Look there he is! You … old man!' Eddy's shout alerted Grandad to his approach, his jeans slipping down delayed his arrival. 'So what's this then?' He shoved Max's drawing in front of Grandad's face. 'You thought you could swindle me?' He bounced on his toes like a boxer warming up. 'Me, Eddy Jost. Don't you know who I am?' He jabbed his fist into the air missing Grandad's face by a few inches. 'No one messes with me! No one! Do you hear me?' He poked Grandad's chest. 'Give me my money and we'll call it quits. Otherwise ...' He followed up with several air jabs.

Grandad, eyes front, never blinked. He watched Eddy's antics with a mixture of sorrow and amusement. Sorrow as he knew he was young and that such behaviour would not lead him to a happy place in years to come. And amusement because with each bounce his trousers slipped further down.

Out of the corner of his eye he saw Max leading two burly policemen over to where they were.

Grandad's silence and lack of retaliation frustrated Eddy further. 'Don't mess with me.' Their faces all but touched. 'Give me my money now!' The veins on his forehead stood out. Losing control he pulled his arm back. He held his clenched fist at shoulder height.

Before he could release a punch, Ticker Wright, with the skill of a champion wrestler, slipped his hand into the crook shape made by Eddy's arm. Following through, he soon had Eddy's head pinned up against the wall, his arms behind his back, legs stretched wide.

'Get off me you great oaf.' Unaware of the police presence Eddy wriggled to break loose. The ratcheting sound of closing hand-cuffs put paid to that. His struggling ceased.

'I have to caution you. You do not have to say anything, but it may harm your defence if you do not mention when questioned, something which you later rely on in court. Anything you do say may be given in evidence. Do you understand?' Ticker said. 'And while you're at it I'd pull my trousers up, otherwise I'll add indecent exposure to the charges.'

The sound of sirens penetrated the gathering of on-lookers.

Billy and Ant heard, as did everyone else.

'Let's take a look.' Ant led. Moving in the direction of the commotion, he jumped onto a bench seat to get a better view. 'Hey look … it's your grandad!'

Billy took off at top speed. Jacko pulled hard on his lead. Billy lost grip. Jacko vanished into the crowd.

'Grandad!' He was stuck behind a line of people all jostling to get a better view, 'I'm here!' Billy's heart thumped in his chest. He pushed with all his might to force his way to the front. He was stopped by a policeman. 'It's my grandad! Please let me see him.'

'Is this your sister?' The policeman was holding Max's hand.

'Yes, no, not really.' Confused Billy just wanted to reach his grandad. 'She's my mate's sister.' He glanced at Max. 'What you doing here?'

'We've got your twenty pound note back from Eddy,' she couldn't get the words out fast enough, 'and Ticker Wright's arrested him.' She pointed towards a handcuffed Eddy, beyond whom he could see Tom, Kate and their mum.

A paramedic tried to examine Grandad. Jacko grabbed the red blanket the man had wrapped around him.

'It's okay boy. He's a friend.' Billy said.

The dog didn't look convinced. He bared his teeth at the medic. Grandad looked overwhelmed. Everything had moved so fast but at least he'd Billy's money back.

8 - THE WRONG TWENTY POUND NOTE

'Billy why didn't you tell us?' His mum said when they were all safely home. 'I know Eddy Jost only too well. He's trouble at school, he's been excluded several times.'

Billy felt pleased to hear this. At least his grandad knew he hadn't lied.

'As for you Grandad,' She went on, 'The Great Magisco, what if he'd have punched you or something? You're too old for capers like that.' She turned to Max who sat at the table tucking into a bowl of her favourite ice cream. 'We have Max here to thank. She saved the day.'

She smiled up at them between spoonful's.

'Oh Billy, before I forget, here's your twenty pounds.' Grandad opened his wallet to remove a pristine note taken straight from a cashpoint machine. 'Now take it up to your bedroom and put it safely away.'

'Thanks Grandad.' He wrapped his arms around him. 'And thanks Max! I'll do it right now'. He ran out of the room heading for the stairs. Before he gone far he let out a cry of anguish. 'Grandad!' He ran back to where they were.

'It's not mine!' He held out the note. The others moved in to get a closer look.

What do you mean it's not yours?' Mum said.

'See, here,' he pointed at it, 'my name is missing. I wrote *BILLY 10 10 10* in black ink on the Queen's neck, just under her chin.' His elation gone, despair returned. No longer upright, he rounded his shoulders and slouched off towards his bedroom. He wanted to be alone.

'Billy, come here … please.' Grandad's voice was calm, 'I need to tell you something.'

'What?'

'Listen to your Grandad Billy.' His mum said. 'I'm sure there's a good reason.'

Billy stood in front of Grandad, his eyes cast to the ground. He didn't want to hear any reason; he just wanted *his* twenty pound note back.

'Eddy Jost is a bad lad.' Grandad looked to his daughter, who nodded in agreement, 'He's in real trouble for what he's done and the police want to take him to juvenile court. To do that they need to ask you and Ant some questions about what happened in the park. Is that clear?' He waited for a response.

Billy muttered.

'Speak up Billy, Grandad can't hear so well.'

'Yes …, can I go now?' He turned to leave. Grandad caught hold of his arm.

'Not yet, I haven't finished. As well as asking you questions, I need to make a statement—that's what the police call it—about what happened. And since the whole thing revolves around your twenty pound note, they've kept it for evidence.'

'What, my twenty pound note? Why?'

'Because it's important.'

'So they'll take fingerprints and put it under one of the machines with a blue light to see if they match Eddy's?' The idea raced away with him. 'Will they have to take my fingerprints? And Ant's?' He inspected his hands trying to decide which one he used to hold the note. 'What about my writing?' He looked to his mum and back to Grandad. 'You know, 'cos I wrote on it. Will I be in trouble for writing on the Queen?'

'Hey slow down Inspector Clouseau.'

'Yeah, but what about Jacko here. He could have touched it!' Jacko sat by Billy. 'Will they want his paw prints?' They looked down at the dog. He raised a paw.

'See he knows …'

'You are a rascal.' Grandad glanced at Billy's mum, 'I see my favourite grandson is back.'

'Does that mean my note's gone forever?' Billy sighed heavily.

'Only until Eddy's been to court … but it might be a while. So in the meantime I've got your new one.' He smiled at Billy. 'You know it doesn't matter about it not being the actual note. What's important is you've the money to spend as you want. Eddy'll have to pay for his actions. Bullying, stealing and threatening behaviour aren't acceptable. Let's hope he's learnt a lesson.' Grandad took hold of his grandson's shoulders. 'Come on Billy lad, smile. It's not so bad.' He tickled his ribs.

Squirming, Billy couldn't stop a laugh escaping. He wriggled to get away. Jacko joined in the fun, barking enthusiastically.

Really Billy wanted *his* twenty pound note to remind him of his once in a life time tenth birthday on the tenth day of the tenth month. But he was more pleased to know he could count on his family and friends in times of trouble. And he still had Grandad's twenty pounds to spend on a special birthday present.

WHAT YOU CAN LEARN FROM THIS STORY

Bullies look confident and strong. That's why they seem scary. They cannot let their guard down because then they would seem less confident and therefore wouldn't be able to bully. So they keep behaving as if they are the most important people on the planet, whilst inside they are just like you and me. They are in fact acting, as if they were on TV. Acting confident and strong. Acting as if they have power over others. And of course, they surround themselves with people who are like them—just in case they need reinforcements! And that's the power of the bully—they are not often on their own. So simply standing your ground and confronting them just makes them even worse because they have to defend their position and the only way they know how to do that is by doing more of what they're already doing.

As in the story, the best way to deal with bullies is to ask for help from people who have more experience in understanding what's happening—in this case Grandad. He knows that to overcome the bullies you have to use a strategy, just like in a computer game. Hatch a plan that will disarm the bully rather than fight them. It may also be important for an adult to get the authorities involved, in this case the police, so the proper action can be taken.

Notice also in the story that Billy felt guilty about having lost the twenty pound note to the bullies, which made him nervous about confessing what had happened. When his Mum asked him if he was okay, he had to lie to her as he was frightened to tell her the truth. Making you feel nervous, anxious or scared gives the bullies more ammunition to try to control you. If Billy could have confided in his mum or grandad straight away, he would have been able to get the help he needed and he wouldn't have had to wait for Maxine to get involved.

It takes courage to deal with difficult situations. Courage comes from within you; it's the knowing that you are the same as everyone else. You can then hold your head high and say with confidence—I am important and I deserve to be treated fairly.

Some interesting quotations:

If you're horrible to me I'm going to write a song about it and you won't like it. That's how I operate. **Taylor Swift**

Courage is fire, and bullying is smoke. **Benjamin Disraeli**

If you have been touched by anything in this book that you're not sure about, please email Maggie at maggie@maggieminter.co.uk for advice or support.

Book Review

If you found this book beneficial leaving a review on Amazon and / or Goodreads would be much appreciated by me and others who have yet to find it. Thank you.

ABOUT THE AUTHOR

James is a full time fiction author, writing for the last five years. Prior to this he spent thirty five years in the IT industry where he wrote many hundreds of training manuals. He turned his attention to fiction during the summer of 2009. Armed with an A4 pad and ballpoint pen he unleashed a stream of consciousness—some forty thousand words—before drawing breath. Writing with such unbridled passion was new to him; a far cry from technical authoring. The excitement of not knowing where the narrative is going spurs him on, as do the characters he invents. **The Hole Opportunity** was the first product of his imagination. **The Unexpected Consequences of Iron Overload** followed a year later. (A paranormal, romantic spoof thriller, written to raise awareness of a genetic medical condition called Haemochromatosis, and to raise funds for the Haemochromatosis Society). Book two of the Hole Trilogy—**A Tunnel is Only a Hole on its Side,** was released in December 2013. James is currently writing book three of the Hole Trilogy—**Marmite Makes a Sandwich, Dynamite Makes a Hole**, and the **Life Lesson Series** whilst continuing to raise awareness for Haemochromatosis. He enjoys sharing experiences of self-publishing and self-promotion with other indie authors.

Website: www.jamesminter.com
E-Mail: james@jamesminter.com **Twitter:** @james_minter
Amazon: http://amzn.com/e/B00735B54U
Facebook: www.facebook.com/author.james.minter

TITLES IN THE LIFE LESSON SERIES

This series of life learning books are written to help parents deal with the issues raised but in a gently way through story telling. Children who read these stories are able to see the issues in an everyday context and so appreciate their meaning and how they might apply to them. These books act as icebreakers between adults and children allowing conversations to be had which start the process of addressing the negative aspects of these behaviours.

Eight books are planned in the series but we welcome any feedback from parents/teachers who would like to see additional topics dealt with in this way. Contact the author by email: james@jamesminter.com

Billy's Tenth Birthday - Bullying
Bullies appear confident and strong. That's why they are scary and intimidating. Billy loses his birthday present of a twenty pound note to the school bully. By involving a grownup he manages to get it back and the bully gets his comeuppance.

Billy and Ant Fall Out - Pride
Pride is something that gets in the way of you being able to choose what you really want to do. It becomes so important that you'd rather do something wrong than admit you have made a mistake. In this story Billy says something nasty to Ant and they row. Ant goes off and makes a new friend. Billy though upset refuses to apologise.

What Billy Knows - Secrets
If something is to be kept a secret there must be a reason and it's usually to protect someone else. This story explores the issues of secret keeping by Billy and Ant.

Billy's Horrible to Ant - Jealousy

Jealousy hurts only the person who feels it. When Billy's friend Ant wins a school prize he can't stop himself saying horrible things. He is envious rather than being pleased for his friend.

Billy and Ant are Late for School - Lying

Lying is normal. It's wrong, but it's normal. Lies are told for a number of different reasons but frequently done to avoid trouble. Billy and Ant mess around while cycling to school and are late. They lie about a flat tyre. As they passed the garage they witness a serious crime and the police come to visit them and their school. Their lie then gets them into trouble!

'Max , you have to put them back' - Stealing

Stealing is taking something from someone else without permission or payment. When children steal it might be for a dare, because they have no money or as a way of getting attention. Stealing shows a lack of self-control. Max sees some go faster stripes for her bike in the shop. She has to have them but her birthday is ages away.

Billy Thinks he's not Good Enough - Self-Belief

It is essential children believe in themselves and their abilities, but having an inflated ego is detrimental. If they don't believe in themselves it's difficult for other to do so. But overpraising isn't helpful. Billy is picked for the lead role in the school play. He is convinced he's not good enough and bound to mess up.

'Go on mum, please buy it for me.' - Value of Money

The value of money is one of the most important subjects for a child to learn and carry with them into adulthood yet it is one of the least taught subjects. Billy and Ant want to their own skateboards but soon realise a reasonable one will cost a significant amount of money.

7835260R00038

Printed in Great Britain
by Amazon.co.uk, Ltd.,
Marston Gate.